HOT *tips for*
COLD *readings*

Some Do's and Don'ts for Actors at Auditions

A Smith and Kraus Book
Published by Smith and Kraus, Inc.
Box 10 Main Street
Newbury, Vermont 05051

Book layout by Anne McArthur.
U.S. Vocabulary introduced by Marisa Smith.
Manufactured in the United States of America

First published in Great Britain in 1992
by Maverick Press, 69 Woodstock Road, London N4 3EU

Library of Congress Cataloging-in–Publication Data
Finburgh, Nina, 1937-
     Cold readings : some do's and don'ts for actors at auditions / by Nina Finburgh ; illustrations by Anne McArthur.
        p. cm.
     ISBN 1-880399-50-4 : $8.95
     1. Acting--Auditions. I. McArthur, Anne, 1949- . II. Title.
     PN2071.A92F56   1993
     792'.028--dc20   93-39770
                                   CIP
                                   AC

CONTENTS

Unprepared Readings

The top of your head is not expressive.

Don't look down at the script all through the reading.

Some people may look like this

or like this

Most of us don't.

Your face is **UNIQUE**.

It expresses what you are feeling or thinking as you read.

Let the director **SEE** it.

The director has studied the scene. Yours may be the 6th reading he has sat through this morning.

He does not need to hear the words perfectly read as if you're on the radio.

LOOK UP

Let him see your unique qualities which he may remember for future roles even if you're not suitable for the one on offer.

Don't be frightened of losing your place.

Keep your thumb in the margin and let it slide down as you read.

THIS IS IMPORTANT.

Knowing your thumb is acting as a marker quickly identifying your place in the text allows you to feel confident about looking up from it.

Don't use your index finger along the text to trace the place. That movement distracts.

Whereas your thumb, slowly moving down the page, cannot be seen from out front.

Your other hand can hold the spine of the book, or is free to express the character's feelings.

Directors often hand you the text <u>then</u> describe the character and situation.

LISTEN

Don't glance at the text trying to sneak a look at the first line.

The director is telling you what she is looking for. Giving you guidelines.

LISTEN

Avoid irrelevant questions.

Nerves make some artists postpone the moment of starting.

They seek reassurance by asking for more information.

You may feel reassured, but remember that directors are often pressed for time.

There is only **ONE** important question for you to ask:
"May I look at it for a moment, please?"
Most directors allow this, but not all.

Presuming the answer is:

Look down at the first few words (keeping your thumb on the margin).

Give yourself time to understand and identify with them.

LOOK UP and **COMMUNICATE** the sense and feeling of them.

In this way: "Hi, Harry" will not just be 'read'.
It will be colored with your own individual quality.

Don't panic while you glance down to see the next 3 or 4 words.

<u>You</u> as the character exist. The silence while you look down is filled with the visual body language of the phrase you have just performed.

See the next few words and go through the process of thinking or feeling their meaning **BEFORE** you speak them

so that.....

"Long time no see".....
can be a reproach

or a mild tease

or just joyous.

When you're doing a cold reading, there is no right or wrong way to speak a line.

At this stage it doesn't matter which way you say it,
AS LONG AS YOU MEAN IT.

12

The director may know how he or she wants it eventually, but now **YOU** are more important than the line.

You are either interesting, or you are not.

Reading "Hi Harry, long time no see"..... with your face in the book is **NOT** interesting.

TRUST YOURSELF!

If you have played "long time no see" joyously and then discover that the next phrase is:-

    "You slimy creep, where's my $5.00?"

Don't panic!

DON'T ask to start again
      or think "Now I've muffed it"
      or feel foolish.

Concentrate on the line.

Play "You slimy creep" positively, and the transition between "long time no see" (joyous) and "You slimy creep" (resentful) will look spontaneous, as though you had just remembered the money.

14

Proceed through the text breaking it up into small units. Memorize them, and think or feel their meaning before speaking.

If you look up and spout words without thought, you will resemble one of those toy dogs in cars with wobbly heads.

Your thought processes are interesting to watch.

Let the director **SEE** them.

Where to Look

Scenes   If you are reading with another actor, most of the
          lines will be communicated to him or her.

          But not all.

Don't be frightened of using the space out front to reveal
your thoughts, especially if the subtext differs from the line.

Family relationships rarely call for eyeball to eyeball confrontation, so check that you are not using the other actor's face just because it's easier to look there.

Try to **PLAY** the scene, open it out using space and movement.

Remember the **RELATIONSHIP** of the characters. This can alert you to the subtext of the scene.

Give yourself enough time to really identify with the text and your instincts will guide your communication.

LISTEN when your partner speaks.
Do not 'switch off' in order to look at your next line.

"I'VE SHOT YOUR FATHER"

Acting is <u>reacting</u> and your silent response is every bit as important as your line, especially in comedy.

If you read ahead, without paying attention to your partner's line, your own is unlikely to be truthfully developed, and you will have lost the opportunity of allowing the director to see your reaction.

Acting proceeds from moment to moment, so

STAY IN PRESENT TIME.

Should your partner have a long chunk, you can glance down during the speech to see his last words.

<u>Then</u> look down to see your own response.

19

Sometimes you will have to read with an ASM or member of the production staff.

This can be unnerving as your cues may be given in a flat, hurried, 'let's get it over with' manner.

TRY NOT TO BE PUT OFF, or feel that you are going 'over the top' if you read expressively.

The director wants to see **YOU** and is aware that circumstances are not ideal.

Practice reading with a muttering friend, so that you are not thrown when this happens.

Resist catching your friend's pace, intonation and overall caution.

Your task at audition is to <u>reveal your potential</u> so let the director see it.

He or she can guide interpretation during rehearsal.

At this stage, your task is to be **INTERESTING** enough to be remembered.

Monologues for the Stage

Sometimes a director will give you 1 or 2 sheets of a script, and ask you to look them over for a few minutes in another room.

Nerves can affect concentration, and some actors find that their eye swims over the text without fully comprehending its meaning.

If you have privacy, speak your lines <u>aloud</u> as this helps to focus concentration.

22

First read for sense, then look for **VARIETY**.

Remember that directors can only learn about your potential range from what you reveal.

"TO CAST OR NOT TO CAST"

If the monologue seems on one level, look in it for **DIFFERING DIMENSIONS.**

If your role seems basically hurt, look for moments when the character could become shocked or angry.

Remember that scheming bastards can be

and that abused wives may become

HAVE COURAGE!

Probably you will have been given only a superficial description of the role you are to read.

It's up to you to use different aspects of yourself throughout the reading.

Don't be frightened of making <u>bold choices</u> which stretch your emotional range, revealing the sensitivity of your vocal technique far more than a careful, cautious reading from which the director learns little about you.

As long as you communicate each phrase with **SINCERITY** (by giving yourself enough time to connect with it before speaking) you will never be 'over the top'.

Being 'over the top' is to do with Falseness, with showing a contrived emotion without going through the process of feeling it.

If you have privacy, rehearse the piece with movement. Avoid getting into business with props -

but do move when <u>your</u> body feels it's right to do so according to the lines.

There's no need to follow detailed stage directions, but it is wise to let a stage director see that you can handle space - especially if your resume is full of recent TV credits.

Read the passage several times, welcoming any new choices which happen as you rehearse.

When you're called in, **TAKE YOUR TIME**.

Move the furniture if you need to, and decide where you are going to place the person your character is addressing.

Because stage directors need a sense of distance, it's unwise to play the script directly to them.

They may need to make notes, and most prefer to be free to watch you rather than having to become involved in the scene.

Choose a place where you can focus
OUT FRONT.

Find a specific spot to relate to (an object near the director or a mark on the wall).

It is important that you decide this **BEFORE YOU START**.

If your eyes keep hovering about each time you look up, your work will seem to lack focus and clarity.

It is much easier to relate to a fixed spot than to vague, undefined space.

Don't place a chair between you and the director and relate to it.

Your work would be seen in profile and much of your impact would be lost.

30

If the text is addressed to the audience, relate out front to a wide semi-circle, contacting the eyes of anyone (either imaginary or real) who may be watching.

If the text requires you to deal with an oven or fridge or bookcase, imagine these things <u>in front</u> of you.

An audition is a chance to be **SEEN**, why turn your back, denying the director the opportunity of seeing your reaction to the props?

Some actors feel safer placing imaginary people and objects behind them.

They feel less exposed, less 'open' to criticism.

Remember a director is
CASTING.
He or she is not criticizing.
She or he is not sitting in
judgment on your right to call
yourself an Actor.

The director is not your parent.

Nor your teacher.

Directors are **not** primarily concerned with fluency.
Or correct pronunciation.

Some actors fear reading because of bad memories from school.

The fast readers may have been praised and expressive ones mocked or accused of 'showing off' by classmates.

THIS IS DIFFERENT!

If you're up for a specific part, you can assume that your agent has checked the physical requirements in advance.

So the director is looking for someone who has the <u>qualities</u> of the role.

She will not mind if you mispronounce Addisababa.

Expect that you may fluff and do **NOT APOLOGIZE**.

Realize that it does not matter, and concentrate fully on the next line to be read.

Do **NOT** go back and correct yourself.
This is boring, unnecessary and spoils the illusion of character.

Real people <u>do</u> stumble over words.

Your momentary stutter may actually enhance the spontaneity of your work.

Should you turn over 2 pages at once, or speak someone else's line - <u>just be yourself</u>.

Ease the atmosphere (perhaps by sending yourself up in some way). **DO NOT GET UPSET**.

Imagine how painful it must be for directors to witness an actor's obvious distress.

If you've had 10-15 minutes to prepare the script you may have learned some part of it. **Beware of becoming glib!**

Even if you've memorized:

"Do you remember when Charlie was 5? He had these funny little legs and he used to splash about in puddles....."

Don't just say the lines. **SPLIT THEM UP.**

"He had these/ (think and remember) funny little legs/ (visualize) and he used to/ (reach for the word) splash about in puddles....."

In ordinary conversation we do pause for thought, so the silences which occur when you look down at the text seem quite natural.

DON'T RUSH

Some actors are so nervous about keeping a director waiting, they 'chip off' the last word of a phrase they are speaking in order to see what is coming next.

The very essence of a phrase "How could you do that?" comes over in maintaining the hurt <u>after</u> you have spoken.

The pain in your eyes is what makes the line seem real. If you look down on - or immediately after - the word 'that', you undermine the integrity of what you have just said.

DON'T RUSH

Take as long as you need to see the next few words. Identify with them, sharing the feelings and thought processes, <u>before</u> you speak.

Get used to **SILENCE**.
It can be deeply revealing.
Don't feel that you exist only when you are speaking lines.

Your thoughts and feelings give life to the lines.
You are not boring!
When you first start looking up from the text, you may feel
that you are being too slow.
There is no need to <u>speak</u> slowly!
Avoid a labored pace.

Practice with a friend and you will see for yourself that their
silences are not 'empty'.
Often they are the most interesting
moments of all.

Much **Comedy** depends on pace.
Looking up every 3 or 4 words may destroy the build-up of conflict, panic or chaos.

Trust your own instincts and with this style of text

LOOK UP LESS OFTEN

but don't bury your head in the book.

Remember the best laughs may come from your character's surprised or outraged reaction.
Let the director see it.

With practice you will get used to breaking up the text. Getting involved with it becomes enjoyable, and people watching you will hardly be aware of the text in your hand.

Looking down at it will seem part of the thought process and you will be giving a <u>performance</u> as opposed to a mechanical reading.

Television Auditions

These may often involve you in reading scenes <u>with</u> the director.

Some directors enjoy this and identify with their role, reading expressively.

Others are embarrassed at attempting to act and opt out by racing through the lines in a factual, journalistic way.

Don't be put off by this.

The director won't be looking at your response while he reads.

Follow his lines in the script, then wait for him to look up before giving your line directly <u>to</u> him.

Most TV directors are used to having actors relate to them. If for some reason it feels wrong, relate to a spot a few inches from his ear.

If the scene you are reading is composed of very short lines, the director may not look up at you at all.

This is frustrating, but always take time to identify with your line, since your voice becomes more expressive when you do.

Usually you are sitting down on these occasions.

Avoid large gestures or messy movement, remembering that the camera catches <u>thought</u>.

Practice on video if you can, checking that your head is not stressing words which should be emphasised vocally.

Keep it confidential.

<u>Videos</u> are often used for <u>Commercial Castings</u>.

Usually there are only a few lines of script so try to learn them if you can.

If you are reading a scene with another actor, find reasons in the text to look away from your partner so that the camera will observe your thoughts and feelings. Do pick up your cues smartly.

You may be asked to introduce yourself, so practice talking to the camera. Give your name, recent experience and representation, looking directly into the lens in a positive, friendly manner.

Some General Hints

If you are given 2 sheets of paper, or you have to <u>turn over</u> the page in a book -

check what is coming on page 2 before speaking the final words of page 1.

This will prevent an awkward handling of:

    "How was I to know ..... (turn over)

.....he was dead?"

If your agent has told you you're up for a bimbo and you
find it's for a nun, don't–
give up
get angry   **THINK POSITIVELY**
go home.

Slip off your 3 inch heels and feel demure as you
read.
You may not get this part, but the director may
remember your quality and invite you to other
auditions.

Don't bluff and pretend to know a famous play if you don't.

There's no shame in admitting that you need to be reminded of it.

The director may tell you what qualities she's seeking as she outlines plot and character.

If the scene is in dialect, try not to let that be your first consideration, since your work will be diminished if you are worrying about vowel sounds.

ACT the scene as well as you can.

You won't get the role if the director prefers to cast authentically, but some companies employ dialect coaches and you might suggest that you would study with one if cast.

You are unlikely to be cast if your reading is hesitant and apologetic because of the dialect.

Read the scene as well as you can.

If you are interesting the director may ask to see you in the years ahead.

Don't be in awe of Shakespeare.

Some actors are so scared of the language that they give equal weight to each word, reducing the text to a dirge.

Practice sight reading passages applying the same principles:

SEE, CONNECT, RELATE

Once you've got the thought, speak it quickly.

You may not understand a word or a pun, but **DON'T** pull agonized faces.

If the director has time, he'll explain, but at audition he's more likely to be interested in <u>you</u> than the interpretation of the text.

Do be **POSTURE CONSCIOUS**.

It doesn't matter if you're reading Checkov in jeans so long as you sit up or stand with your weight on both feet.

Men   A turn out from the hip will help give a Restoration quality.

Women   Don't cross your legs at the knee before 1920 approx.

"I AM A SEAGULL"

Sit up on the chair. <u>Don't slouch</u> with your elbows on your knees.

You may feel more secure and less exposed, but your body language is restricted from this position and your authority is diminished.

Do make sure that your hair is not masking your face.

If you're asked to read in a different way, it's not a criticism of your performance, it's a compliment!

The director is prepared to spend more time with you.

He or she may have liked your first interpretation, but now needs to learn how adaptable you are.

Do be sure to look up on the first phrase of text - whatever the style.

The impact you make should start <u>at the top</u>.

Don't be casual unless the text specifically requires it.

Asking yourself

'What does this character have at stake?'

can help to assess your degree of commitment.

58

If you are seriously dyslexic, it might be wise to warn the director that you may be a bit slow.

This usually evokes sympathy and understanding.

Try to relax and take enough time to make the script your own. Think of the character's situation, and do not monitor your own reading with self-critical judgments.

Glasses can be an asset if used creatively during a reading, but do avoid thick frames which can obscure your facial expressions.

In Conclusion

PRACTICE!

Monologue books are quite useful for this as you can read the same extract as different characters.

Enjoy indulging the text and feeling in control of your own timing.

Practice scenes from the classics with a friend. It's a good way of becoming familiar with the demands of differing styles.

PRACTICE TALKING ABOUT YOURSELF

The questions:

'Tell me about yourself'
or 'What have you been doing recently?'

are almost inevitable.

Go through your credit list <u>before</u> the audition, selecting which jobs are likely to be of most interest to the person you are meeting.

"WELL I'VE BEEN DOING A BIT IN THE GARDEN"

62

Stick to facts.

The name of the play, company and your part, where you played, for how long, and who directed it.

Listening to a detailed description of the plot is less likely to interest the director than hearing about the role you played.

But saying 'I played the lead in Curly McDimple' isn't very helpful!

Try to define characters in a few words, mentioning any change or development throughout the piece.

You don't have to stick to chronological order.
Talk about the role which is most appropriate to the one being cast.

Don't diminish your experience by saying
   'It was only a small part, just a few lines'.
You weren't asked about the size of the role!
Say what you did and enjoyed about it.

You may be up for a tour or a season, and directors aren't likely to warm to actors who complain about poor conditions or direction.

Try to remember that the directors are taking a risk if they don't know your work.

Your posture, manner and interest in the project are all important ingredients of the impression you make.

Rather than hoping that you will be helped to feel at ease, realize that it's the other way round.

It's up to <u>you</u> to help the director feel safe in your competence.

NINA FINBURGH works as consultant to a wide range of performers, including both inexperienced and established actors, along with opera singers, dancers, poets and pop stars.

She has taught at RADA and for the past 10 years has given weekly workshops on Sight Reading and Presentation at the Actors Centre in London.

She has recently returned from Australia where she was invited to introduce her Method of Sight Reading to actors in Sydney and Melbourne.

ANNE McARTHUR has a long track record of work in theatre, including personal experience of auditions, but over the past couple of years has strayed in the direction of layout, design and graphics using her Applemac computer. The illustrations in this book however were perpetrated by more primitive methods.